T0384210

A LLAMA IS NOT AN ALPACA

AND OTHER MISTAKEN ANIMAL IDENTITIES

WRITTEN BY
KAREN JAMESON

ILLUSTRATED BY
LORNA SCOBIE

RP|KIDS
PHILADELPHIA

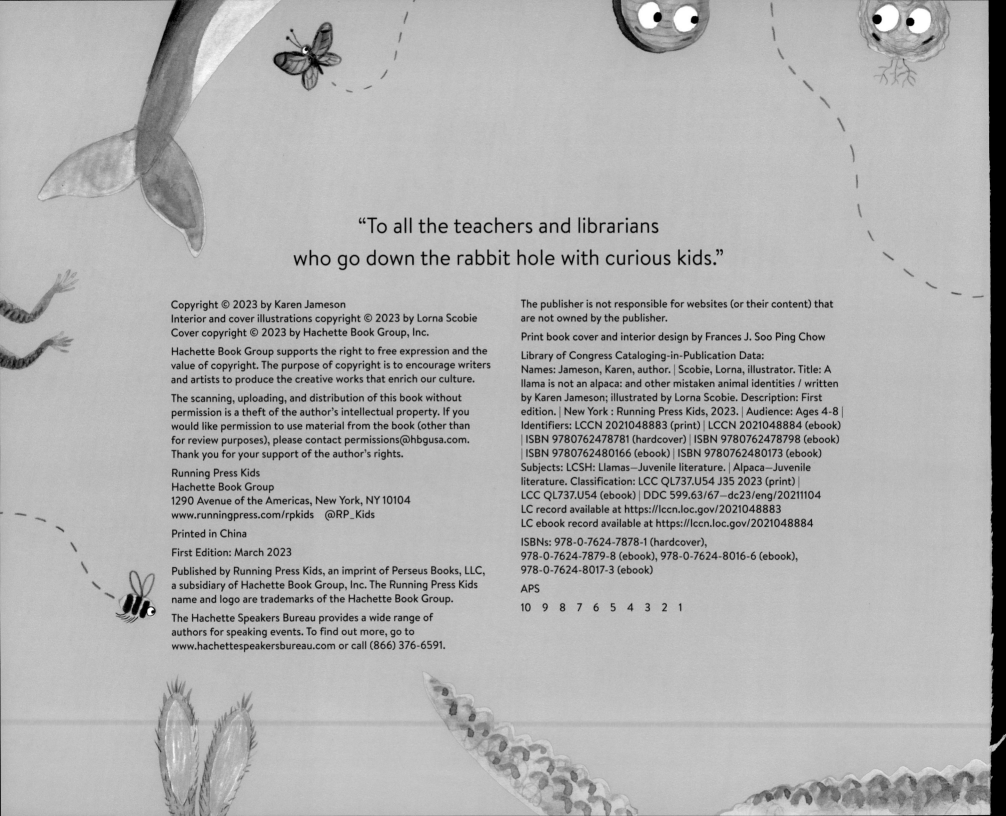

"To all the teachers and librarians
who go down the rabbit hole with curious kids."

Copyright © 2023 by Karen Jameson
Interior and cover illustrations copyright © 2023 by Lorna Scobie
Cover copyright © 2023 by Hachette Book Group, Inc.

Hachette Book Group supports the right to free expression and the value of copyright. The purpose of copyright is to encourage writers and artists to produce the creative works that enrich our culture.

The scanning, uploading, and distribution of this book without permission is a theft of the author's intellectual property. If you would like permission to use material from the book (other than for review purposes), please contact permissions@hbgusa.com. Thank you for your support of the author's rights.

Running Press Kids
Hachette Book Group
1290 Avenue of the Americas, New York, NY 10104
www.runningpress.com/rpkids   @RP_Kids

Printed in China

First Edition: March 2023

Published by Running Press Kids, an imprint of Perseus Books, LLC, a subsidiary of Hachette Book Group, Inc. The Running Press Kids name and logo are trademarks of the Hachette Book Group.

The Hachette Speakers Bureau provides a wide range of authors for speaking events. To find out more, go to www.hachettespeakersbureau.com or call (866) 376-6591.

The publisher is not responsible for websites (or their content) that are not owned by the publisher.

Print book cover and interior design by Frances J. Soo Ping Chow

Library of Congress Cataloging-in-Publication Data:
Names: Jameson, Karen, author. | Scobie, Lorna, illustrator. Title: A llama is not an alpaca: and other mistaken animal identities / written by Karen Jameson; illustrated by Lorna Scobie. Description: First edition. | New York : Running Press Kids, 2023. | Audience: Ages 4-8 | Identifiers: LCCN 2021048883 (print) | LCCN 2021048884 (ebook) | ISBN 9780762478781 (hardcover) | ISBN 9780762478798 (ebook) | ISBN 9780762480166 (ebook) | ISBN 9780762480173 (ebook) Subjects: LCSH: Llamas—Juvenile literature. | Alpaca—Juvenile literature. Classification: LCC QL737.U54 J35 2023 (print) | LCC QL737.U54 (ebook) | DDC 599.63/67—dc23/eng/20211104
LC record available at https://lccn.loc.gov/2021048883
LC ebook record available at https://lccn.loc.gov/2021048884

ISBNs: 978-0-7624-7878-1 (hardcover),
978-0-7624-7879-8 (ebook), 978-0-7624-8016-6 (ebook),
978-0-7624-8017-3 (ebook)

APS

10 9 8 7 6 5 4 3 2 1

Come along on nature hikes
to search for favorite look-alikes.
Study each and every clue.
Don't let these doubles outfox you!

Is this a rabbit or a hare?
Check the ears out to compare.

IT'S A HARE!

HARE VS RABBIT:
Hop to it! Hares are bigger and have longer ears. Their large hind legs move quickly to outrun predators. They live and nest above ground, while most rabbits nest underground.

Butterfly or moth in flight?
One's a creature of the night.

IT'S A MOTH!

BUTTERFLY VS MOTH:
Wings a flutter! Most moths are fly-by-nights, while most butterflies are active during the day.
Drab-colored moths rest with open wings, while colorful butterflies close their wings at naptime.

Clam or oyster? Hard to tell?
Can you find the rougher shell?

IT'S AN OYSTER!

CLAM VS OYSTER:
Surf's up! Oysters have a rough shell, while clam shells are smoother by comparison.
Oysters settle in one spot, while clams move around on one foot. Only oysters make pearls.

Turtle or tortoise? Got you beat?
Guess who paddles with webbed feet.

TURTLE VS TORTOISE:
Slow and steady! Most turtles have webbed feet for swimming, although sea turtles have flippers. Tortoises are land dwellers with short, stubby feet.

Frog or toad now hopping in?
Look for thick and bumpy skin.

IT'S A TOAD!

FROG VS TOAD:
Croak! Most toads have lumpy-bumpy skin
and most frogs have smooth, moist skin.
Frogs are long-legged jumpers compared
to the short-legged toad.

Puffin? Penguin in the sky?
Which seabird can really fly?

IT'S A PUFFIN!

PUFFIN VS PENGUIN:

Waddle, waddle! Weighing just over a pound, puffins are light enough for flight.
The penguin is just too heavy, but its wings make awesome flippers for swimming underwater.

Alpaca? Llama? Big surprise.
One of them comes SUPERSIZE!

ALPACA VS LLAMA:
Lickety-spit! Llamas are almost twice the size of alpacas and have longer, curved ears.
Alpacas have shorter ears and chubby, furry faces. Both like to spit!

Porpoise? Dolphin swimming in?
Which one has a curvy fin?

IT'S A DOLPHIN!

PORPOISE VS DOLPHIN:
Splish, splash! As a dolphin crests a wave, you can see
its curved dorsal fin. A porpoise fin is shaped like a triangle.
The dolphin has a longer beak, too.

Croc or gator? Be a sleuth.
Guess who grins from tooth to tooth?

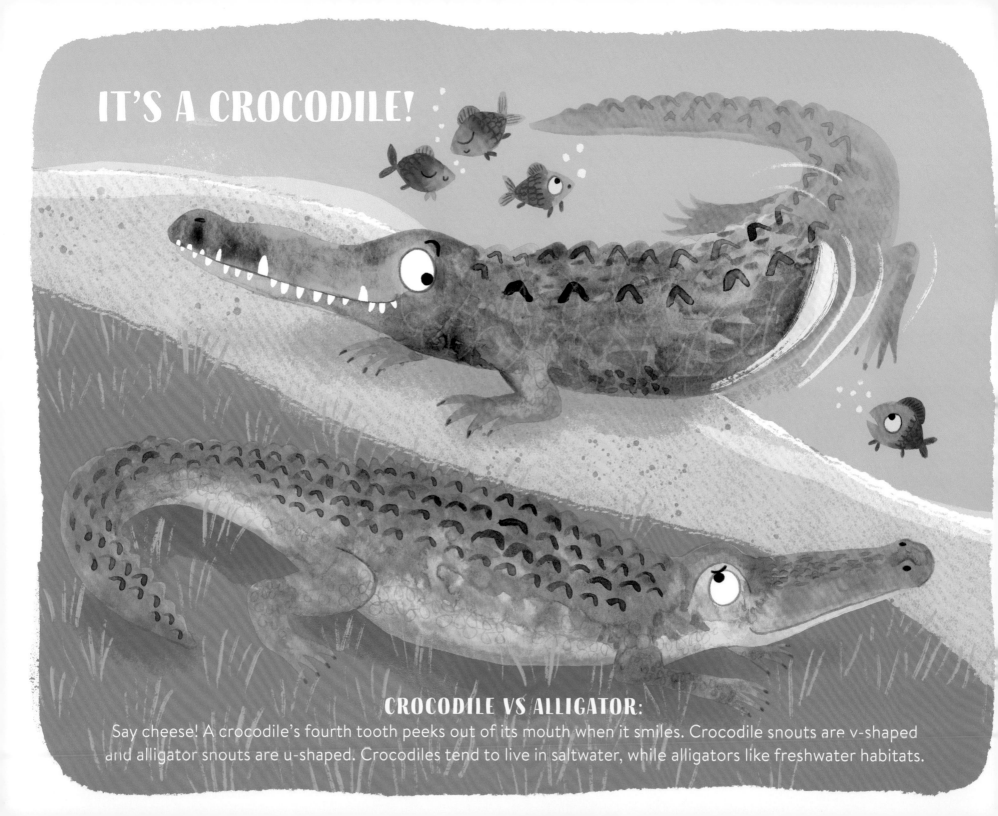

IT'S A CROCODILE!

CROCODILE VS ALLIGATOR:

Say cheese! A crocodile's fourth tooth peeks out of its mouth when it smiles. Crocodile snouts are v-shaped and alligator snouts are u-shaped. Crocodiles tend to live in saltwater, while alligators like freshwater habitats.

Triple dare! Wasp, hornet, bee?
Who's the roundest of the three?

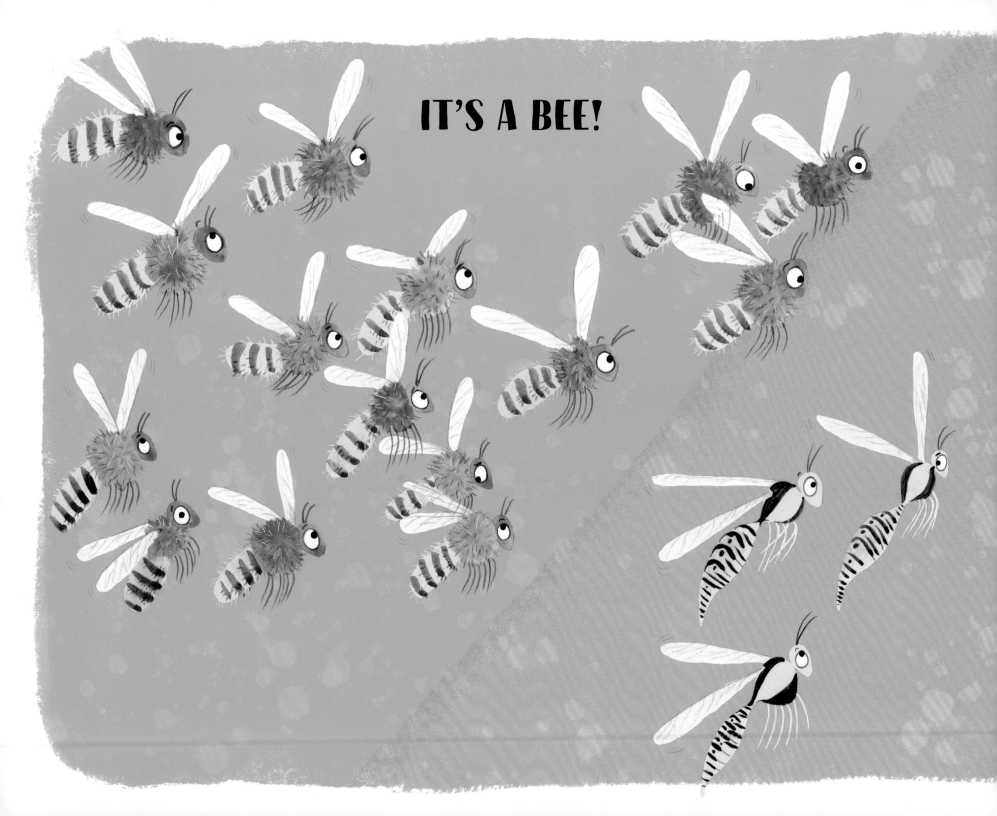

IT'S A BEE!

WASP VS HORNET VS BEE:

Here's the buzz! The bee is the roundest and hairiest. Pollen sticks to its fuzzy body.
Wasps have shiny, slender bodies. Hornets are a larger type of wasp with a bigger head.

Who mastered each and every clue?
Results are in. The winner's YOU!